RAPTORS

VULTURES

JULIE K. LUNDGREN

ROURKE PUBLISHING

Vero Beach, Florida 32964

www.rourkepublishing.com

Project Assistance:
The author also thanks raptor specialist Frank Taylor and the team at Blue Door Publishing.

Photo credits: Cover © ostromec; Title Page © Brooke Whatnall; Contents Page © Jan Coetzee; Page 4 © Nick Biemans; Page 5 © Eric Gevaert; Page 7 © Damian Gil, Pyshnyy Maxim Vjacheslavovich; Page 8 © Kitch Bain; Page 9 © Paul Banton; Page 10 © Starks; Page 11 © Sidnei Dantas; Page 12 © Eduard Kyslynskyy; Page 13 © nialat; Page 14 © Colette3; Page 15 © David T Gomez; Page 16 © Eric Isselée; Page 17 © Ewan Chesser; Page 18 © Ali Taylor; Page 19 © Luis César Tejo; Page 20 © Condor 36; Page 21 © George Lamson; Page 22 © E.G.Pors

Editor: Meg Greve

Cover and page design by Nicola Stratford, Blue Door Publishing

Library of Congress Cataloging-in-Publication Data

Lundgren, Julie K.
  Vultures / Julie K. Lundgren.
     p. cm. -- (Raptors)
  Includes index.
  ISBN 978-1-60694-396-0 (hard cover)
  ISBN 978-1-60694-774-6 (soft cover)
  1. Vultures--Juvenile literature. I. Title.
  QL696.F32L868 2010
  598.9'2--dc22
                                        2009000529

Printed in the USA
CG/CG

www.rourkepublishing.com - rourke@rourkepublishing.com
Post Office Box 643328 Vero Beach, Florida 32964

Contents

VULTURE CULTURE

Raptors, or birds of **prey**, eat other animals. Vultures are a kind of raptor. Raptors also include hawks, eagles, and owls. Unlike these raptors, vultures do not kill their own food. Instead they find and eat dead animals, known as carrion.

King vultures have bumpy, colorful faces. Their beaks can rip open the tough skin of dead animals.

RAPTOR REPORT

IMPORTANT

Considered ugly by many, vulture beauty lies in their graceful, effortless flight.

Old World vultures live in Africa, southern Asia, and southern Europe. Bird scientists consider them true raptors. New World vultures live in North and South America. Even though they look and act like Old World vultures, they are more closely related to storks.

Though often silent, Old World vultures can squeal, whistle, croak, or chitter when excited, such as when feeding. New World vultures have no voice box. They can only grunt or hiss.

Andean condors, the largest of the New World vultures, have wings that measure 12 feet (3.6 meters) from tip to tip.

CLEANING UP

Vulture bodies have special **adaptations** for eating dead animals. They use their sharp beaks to tear meat. After a messy meal, vultures carefully clean their feathers and bodies. Featherless heads and wide nostrils make this task easier.

Vulture feet have less gripping power than other raptors. Other raptors catch live prey, while vultures do not.

This Old World vulture uses its long neck to reach inside the bodies of dead animals.

9

Both New and Old World vultures, like these African white-backed vultures, eat in groups.

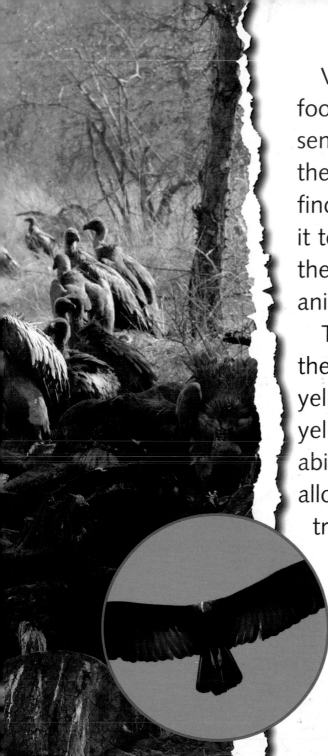

Vultures search great distances for food each day. Most have a poor sense of smell, and instead rely on their excellent eyesight. Once they find a possible meal, they circle over it to get a better view. One reason they do this is to make sure the animal is truly dead.

Three kinds of New World vultures: the turkey vulture, the greater yellow-headed vulture, and the lesser yellow-headed vulture, have the ability to smell rotting meat. This allows them to live in forests, where trees and plants may hide food from sight.

Greater yellow-headed vultures find food by both sight and smell, a rare ability in birds.

11

Once vultures find food, they gulp it down to be sure they get their share. Germs thrive on rotten meat. Vulture stomachs contain strong **acid** that helps kill bacteria and viruses in their food.

Vultures warm up and kill germs on their feathers by opening their wings and soaking up the Sun's rays. Vultures often live in places without much water. They take a solar shower instead!

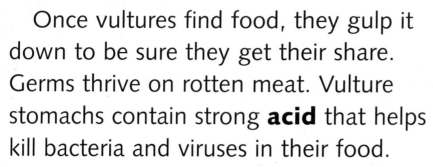

Egyptian vultures use stones to break open ostrich eggs. They eat carrion and live prey.

RAPTOR REPORT
IMPORTANT
IMPORTANT

Bits of food on this turkey vulture's feathers dry in the Sun and fall off, keeping the bird clean and healthy.

Raising Young

Old World vultures generally build stick nests in trees, caves, or on cliffs in **colonies**. New World vultures use cliff nests or hidden grassy nests on the ground. Depending on the kind of vulture, they lay one to three eggs. Both vulture parents care for the eggs and young.

Griffon vultures get their name from the **mythical** griffin, a beast that is part eagle and part lion. Griffon vultures look as if they have a lion's mane.

RAPTOR REPORT

IMPORTANT

Vultures often use the same nests each year. A white-headed vulture in Africa looks over this stick nest.

15

Vulture feet are too weak to carry food to the nest. Instead, they **regurgitate** their last meal to feed their hungry chicks. Young chicks wear a coat of downy feathers and cannot fly. After a few weeks, flight feathers begin growing.

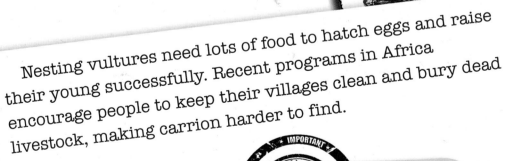

Nesting vultures need lots of food to hatch eggs and raise their young successfully. Recent programs in Africa encourage people to keep their villages clean and bury dead livestock, making carrion harder to find.

RAPTOR REPORT

Young vultures exercise their newly feathered wings to gain strength.

These white-backed vultures clean up the leftovers of an African buffalo.

18

A Bad Name

Because vultures eat dead animals, they have earned a bad name as disgusting and dirty pests. Their large size makes them easy hunting targets. **Scavengers** help people by eating dead animals that might cause disease.

Vultures dining on road kill put themselves in danger from passing cars.

Vulture Future

Sometimes, people take daring steps to bring animals back from the edge of **extinction**. In 1982, only 22 California condors survived. With a rescue plan in place, condor experts captured all wild California condors and helped them nest and raise young under protection.

Many years and millions of dollars later, rescuers carefully released California condors back into the wild, a few at a time. The number of California condors topped 325 in 2008.

Wild California condors live in and around Grand Canyon National Park in northern Arizona.

21

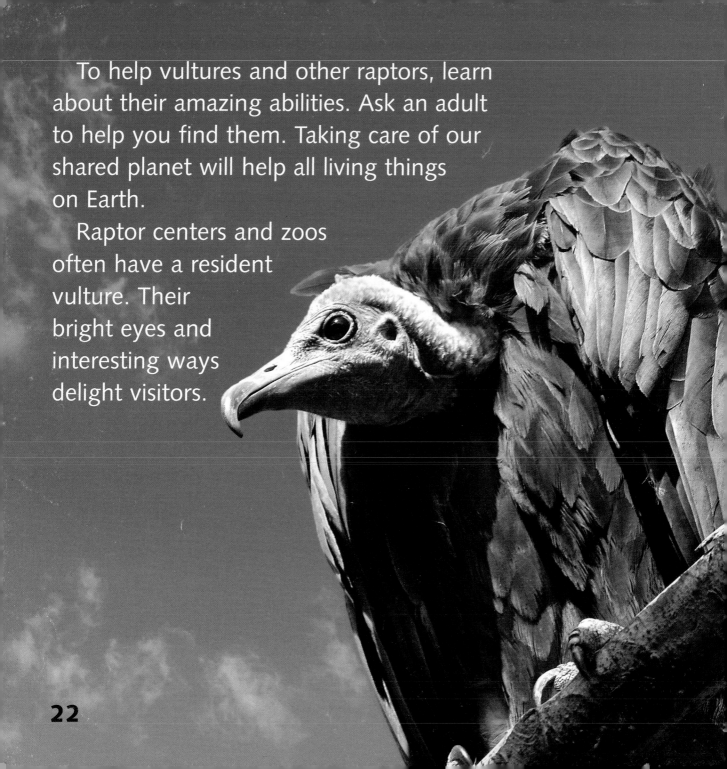

To help vultures and other raptors, learn about their amazing abilities. Ask an adult to help you find them. Taking care of our shared planet will help all living things on Earth.

Raptor centers and zoos often have a resident vulture. Their bright eyes and interesting ways delight visitors.

GLOSSARY

acid (ASS-id): a substance that causes the breakdown of things it touches

adaptations (ad-ap-TAY-shunz): ways of survival that animals and plants have that help them succeed in the place they live

colonies (KOL-uh-neez): groups of animals that nest in one area, usually with greater success than nesting alone

extinction (ek-STINGKT-shun): the complete loss of a species of plant or animal from the Earth

mythical (MITH-i-kuhl): legendary, from folk tales of ancient times

prey (PRAY): animals that are hunted and eaten by other animals

regurgitate (ree-GUR-juh-tate): bring up swallowed, partly digested food to the mouth

scavengers (SKAV-uhn-jerz): animals that eat carrion

Index

Websites to Visit

Soar over to your local library to learn more about vultures and other raptors. Hunt down the following websites:

http://animaldiversity.ummz.umich.edu

www.hawk-conservancy.org

www.hmana.org

www.nps.gov/grca/naturescience/california-condors.htm

www.peregrinefund.org/explore_raptors/

About The Author

Julie K. Lundgren grew up near Lake Superior where she reveled in mucking about in the woods and expanding her rock collection. Her interest in nature led her to a degree in biology and eight years of volunteer work at The Raptor Center at the University of Minnesota. She currently lives in Minnesota with her husband and two sons.